By Tony Tallarico

7004 N. California Ave.
Chicago, IL. 60645

Manufactured in the United States of America

ANSWERS ON LAST PAGE

It's early in the morning and lots of Freddies are waiting for the bus. Can you find the only two Freddies that are exactly alike?

HE LOOKS FAMILIAR!
HE LOOKS LIKE YOU!
I NEVER SAW HIM BEFORE!
I SAW HIM THIS MORNING WHEN I WAS SHAVING!
WE'RE BETTER LOOKING!
I'M HUNGRY!
WHAT ARE WE DOING HERE? TODAY IS OUR DAY OFF!!
MY LETTER STANDS FOR *FISH*!

Freddie sees his name written all over the clouds. Can you find Freddie's name there at least 13 times?

FREDDIE
FREDDIE
FREDDIE
FRED
FREDDIE
FREDDIE
FREDDIE
FREDDIE
CAUTION: LOW CLOUDS
DO NOT CLIMB DOWN!
ONE WAY ONLY

Freddie is looking at this scene through a telescope. Find the following things that he sees:

Anchor
Bat
Fish (6)
Flying bird
Hammer
Horn
Mermaid
Rabbit
Stars (4)
Turtles (3)

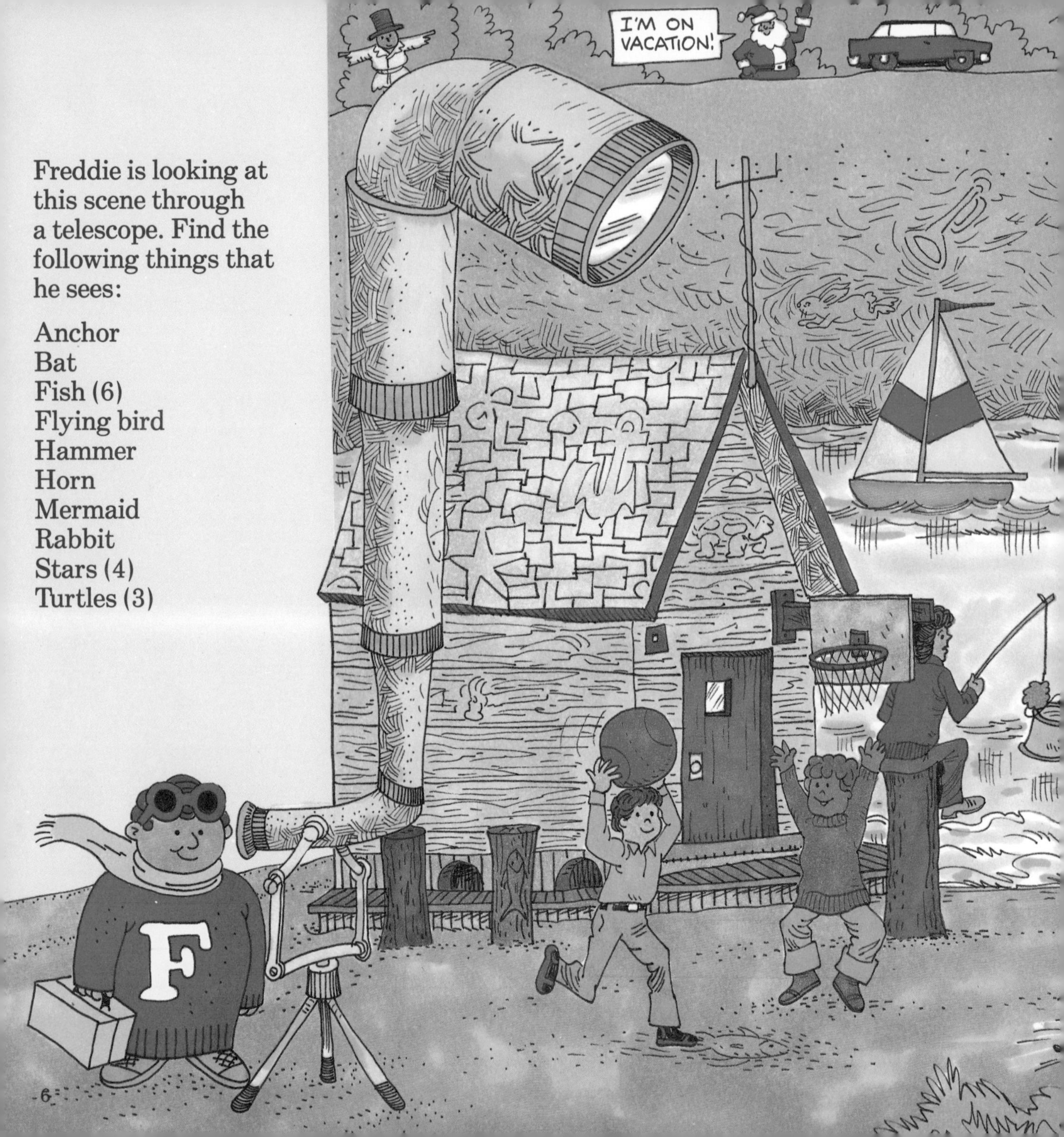

AHOY, SHIP!!
AHOY, WHALE.
?
I WANT TO HUG YOU!
IT'S NOT MY SIZE!
QUACK! QUACK!

These two Freddies look exactly the same. Or do they? Look carefully and find at least eight things that are different between them.

F
F

Freddie has found a birthday party for a famous witch. She is celebrating her 13th. birthday...for the 13th. time!

Find Freddie and the following things:

Arrow
Bats (3)
Bird
Bones (2)
Books (2)
Cupcake
Fish
Heart
Hot dog
Piggy bank
Purse
Straw
Umbrella

I'M LATE!
I WANT SOME CAKE, TOO!
YOU'RE NEXT!
?
NO EXIT
GO FOR IT!
PUFF!
SHE DOESN'T LOOK HER AGE!
YUM!! THE CAKE LOOKS GREAT!
SHE DOESN'T LOOK A DAY OVER 13!
GAIN!
SHE HAS BAD BREATH!
THIS IS A REAL HEART!

PLAY THE FREDDIE TOSS GAME

1. Place the opened book on the floor about five feet away.
2. Each player gets to toss three coins at the open book.
3. Whenever a player's coin lands on an area that has a picture of Freddie, the player receives one point.
4. The first player to get 12 points wins.
5. Be careful. There are "take-away" point zones.
6. Have fun!

TAKE-AWAY
1
POINT ZONE
TAKE-AWAY
3
POINT ZONE

Can you find at least 15 things in this picture that start with the letter *F?*

I'M HUNGRY.

Help Freddie get to the other side of this trail by leading him through the numbers that add up to exactly <u>20</u>.

SHOE!
FLEW!
CLUE!
GLUE!
STEW!
WHO!
BLUE!
Z
HELLO, FREDDIE!
20

Freddie is spending a day at the beach. What's wrong here? Before he goes into the water, help Freddie find at least twelve things that are wrong with this picture.

?
ULP!
DROP THE ANCHOR.

You can always count on Freddie. Now, Freddie is counting on you to find the following:

Automobile (1)
Kites (2)
People (3)
Stars (4)
Balloons (5)
Rabbits (6)
Ducks (7)
Flowers (8)
Envelopes (9)
Birds (10)

N
E
W
S
COUNTING
ZONE
F

Help astronaut Freddie get back to Earth by traveling through this space maze, while finding lots of things along the way.

BLAST OFF!

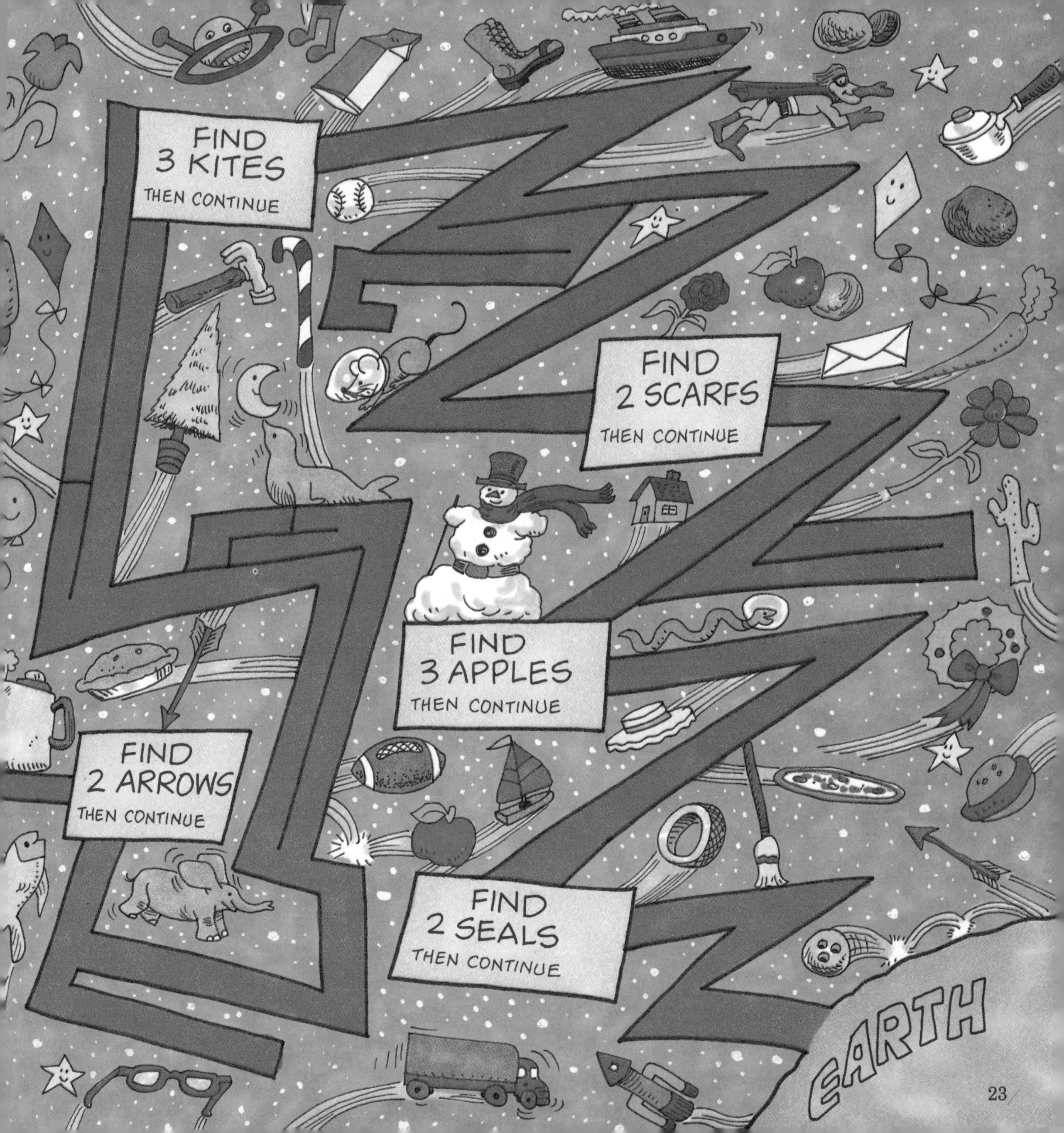
FIND
3 KITES
THEN CONTINUE
FIND
2 SCARFS
THEN CONTINUE
FIND
3 APPLES
THEN CONTINUE
FIND
2 ARROWS
THEN CONTINUE
FIND
2 SEALS
THEN CONTINUE
EARTH

ANSWERS

2-3

4-5

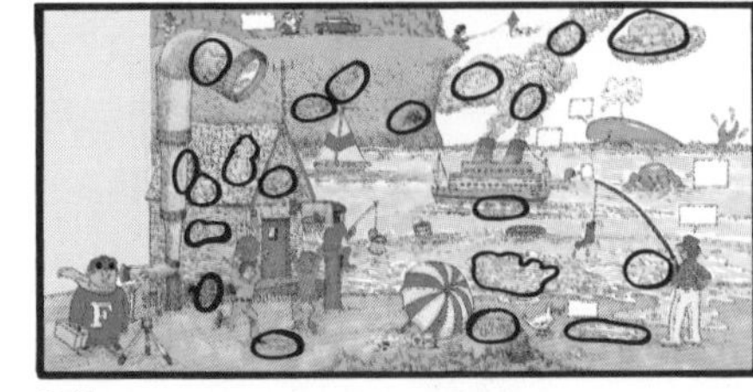
6-7

8-9

10-11

14-15

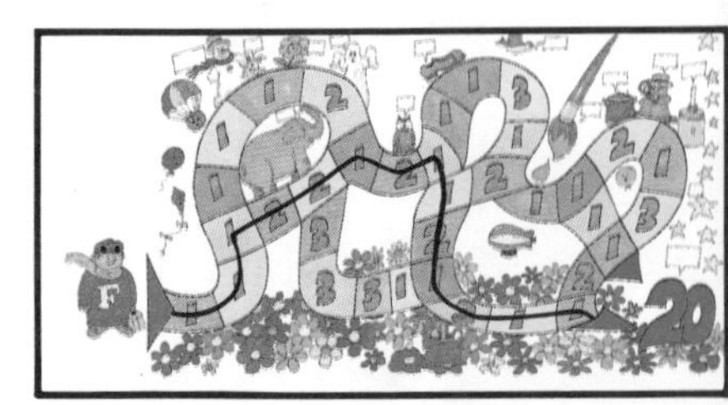
16-17

18-19

20-21

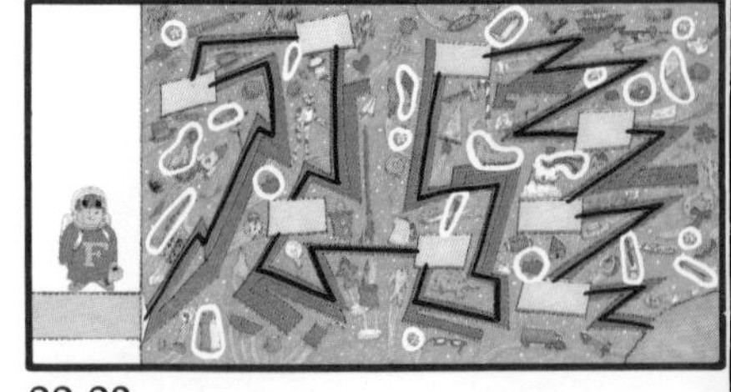
22-23